Our Global Community

Farming

Cassie Mayer

Heinemann
LIBRARY

www.heinemann.co.uk/library
Visit our website to find out more information about Heinemann Library books.

To order:
 Phone 44 (0) 1865 888066
Send a fax to 44 (0) 1865 314091
 Visit the Heinemann Bookshop at www.heinemann.co.uk/library to browse our
catalogue and order online.

First published in Great Britain by Heinemann Library, Halley Court, Jordan Hill, Oxford OX2 8EJ, part of Harcourt Education. Heinemann is a registered trademark of Harcourt Education Ltd.

Editorial: Diyan Leake
Design: Joanna Hinton-Malivoire
Picture research: Ruth Smith
Production: Duncan Gilbert

Origination: Chroma Graphics (Overseas) Pte Ltd
Printed and bound in China by South China Printing Company Ltd

ISBN 978 0 431 19104 1
11 10 09 08 07
10 9 8 7 6 5 4 3 2 1

British Library Cataloguing in Publication Data
Mayer, Cassie
Farming. - (Our global community)
1. Agriculture - Juvenile literature
I. Title
630

Acknowledgements
The publishers would like to thank the following for permission to reproduce photographs: Alamy pp. **7** (Foodfolio), **13** (Sue Wilson); Corbis pp. **4**, **5** (Scott Sinklier), **6** (Stuart Westmorland), **9** (Michael S. Yamashita), **9** (Gary Houlder), **10** (Christine Osborne), **11** (Hein van den Heuvel/zefa), **12** (Ed Young), **14** (Thierry Prat/Sygma), **15** (Alison Wright), **16** (Wolfgang Kaehler), **17** (Margaret Courtney-Clarke), **18** (Randy Wells), **19** (B.S.P.I.), **20** (Keren Su), **21** (aldrin Xhemaj/epa), **22** (Frans Lanting), **23** (Randy Wells; aldrin Xhemaj/epa; Wolfgang Kaehler).

Cover photograph of a farmer ploughing a field in Peru, South America reproduced with permission of Corbis/Keren Su.

Every effort has been made to contact copyright holders of any material reproduced in this book. Any omissions will be rectified in subsequent printings if notice is given to the publishers.

Contents

Farming around the world........ 4

Growing crops 6

Keeping animals 14

How farmers work the land 18

Picture glossary 23

Index 24

Farming around the world

All around the world, people grow food on farms.

A person who farms is called
a farmer.

Growing crops

wheat

Crops are plants that farmers grow.
Some farmers grow wheat.

The wheat is made into flour.

We make bread with the flour.

rice

Some farmers grow rice.

Rice grows in a paddy field.

We eat the grains of rice.

bananas

Some farmers grow fruit.
Bananas grow in hot places.

apples

Apples grow in cool places.

radishes

Some farmers grow vegetables.

Vegetables are good for you to eat.

Keeping animals

Some farmers keep cows for milking.

We drink the milk from cows.

wool

Some farmers keep sheep for their wool.

wool

The wool is used to make clothes.

How farmers work the land

Some farmers use big machines to work the land.

Some farmers use small machines
to work the land.

Some farmers use animals to work the land.

Some farmers use hand tools to work the land.

All around the world, farmers use the land to grow food.

Picture glossary

 **machine** something that helps you do a job more easily

 **tool** something that you use with your hands to make work easier

 **wool** fur of a sheep. We use wool to make jumpers.

Index

bread 7

cows 14, 15

flour 7

fruit 10

machines 18, 19, 23

milk 15

rice 8, 9

sheep 16, 23

tools 21, 23

vegetables 12, 13

wheat 6, 7

wool 16, 17, 23

Notes for parents and teachers

Before reading

Ask the children if they have ever visited a farm. What animals did they see on the farm? What machinery did they see? Look at pictures, posters, and books about farms. Explain that there are farms all over the world and that they grow different crops and rear different animals.

After reading

Farm animal noises. Sing "Old Macdonald Had a Farm" and encourage the children to make the animal noises. Make pairs of cards, each with a farm animal, and give these out to the children. Explain that they are to move around the room making the noise of their animal and to find the other person who has the same animal. When they find their partner, they should sit down. Swap cards and play again.

Food from farms. Show the children some wheat (or show them a picture of wheat), flour, and bread. Explain that the wheat is ground into flour and then baked into bread. Do the same with rice. Show them a picture of the rice plant and some grains of rice. If possible cook the rice or show the children some cooked rice.